# Bloodstream Is An Illusion
# Of Rubies Counting Fireplaces

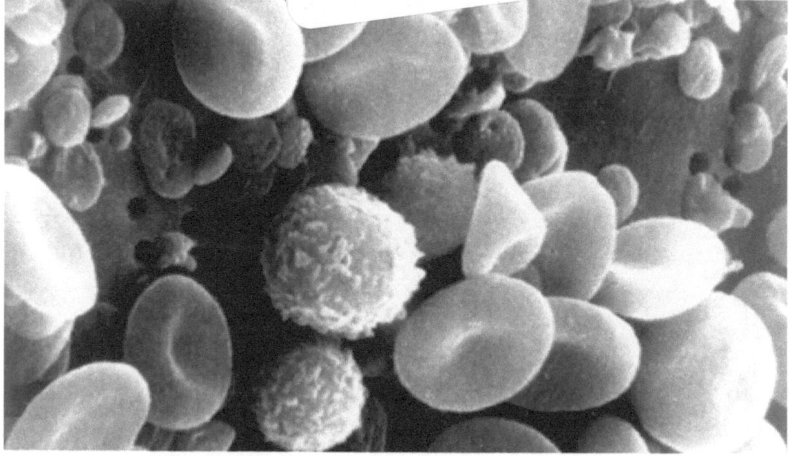

**100 Poems
by Peter J. Dellolio**

Cyberwit.net
HIG 45 Kaushambi Kunj, Kalindipuram
Allahabad - 211011 (U.P.) India
http://www.cyberwit.net
Tel: +(91) 9415091004
E-mail: info@cyberwit.net




Printed at VCORE.

# Contents

# BLURRY SKETCHES

Blurry
sketches
escaped
the
elegant
lamp
looking for the shaking hand
that
made
them.

# MISCHIEF

Mischief
wound
into
a
glowing
bronze
fox head.

Keep
the
window
shut:
the head tries to jump out at night.

It hears
the laughing magician
handing out boxes
of cleverness.

# PENGUINS CONFUSED

Penguins
confused
by thousands of
large salt and pepper shakers.

# TO TAKE THE ANGER

To take the anger
out of splinters
flying into palms
one must cover
a
staircase with thick soft mud.

Silent, smooth, soothing.

# THE FACELESS DUMMIES

The faceless dummies stole
a big old radio.  Gathered in
a circle around it, they
waited for news reports
of their theft.  A bird
turned the knob to a
big band station.

# AN AVALANCHE

An avalanche of
vests
but somehow all the
buttons reassembled in
vertical rows.

The waterfall had
crooked bow ties
and was jealous.

# THE LOCOMOTIVE

The locomotive resents
loosing all of that
sensuous curling steam
and smoke.

It's like *Rapunzel*
cruelly wrapping *Samson's*
bald head with her
long locks.

# THE ALARM CLOCKS

The alarm clocks washed all the
blood off the guillotine
blade.

Another execution is scheduled
for 6am.

# THEY HEARD HYSTERICAL LAUGHTER

They heard hysterical laughter
inside the pointy wizard hat.

Many cheerful children were
grouped around it, eating ice
cream and poking one another.

The adults shook their heads
and moved on.

# MACHINERY SHADOWS

Machinery shadows.
Foamy wake.
Ascending birthday candle smoke.

There is a voice
in the "afterwards"
of things.  It speaks
gracefully of us.

Even the sliding grave dirt
caressing coffins.

# THE FACE OF THE BANJO

The face of the banjo.
White coconut pie.
Thin strands of licorice run across it.

Over in the corner is the baker
in an old wooden phone booth,
stolen recipes jumping out of his pockets.

# THE CRABS

The crabs stoically marched towards the
lighthouse.  It was debated and
they took a vote.  Now they
would present their case to the
lighthouse keeper.  "Could you
please allow a few ships to
crash against the rocks?" they
asked in unison.  "We're tired
of eating seaweed!"

# BLOODSTREAM IS AN ILLUSION OF RUBIES COUNTING FIREPLACES

Bloodstream is an illusion of
rubies counting fireplaces.

Moonlight is the ghost of a
gray bath.

Silk is the beginning of a
hesitant prayer.

# IF THERE IS A LAUGHING CLOWN

If there is a laughing clown
hidden deep inside the burning
orange glow of the lantern,
all of the animals have escaped
and their fur is matted with
            blood.

# THE CREVICE

The crevice zealously guards the
emptiness that it frames.

There are no flaws or derelictions
of duty.

If there were, who would want
to look in?

# HOAX

Hoax in the romantic summer
night at the drive-in.

Someone running around in a rubber
monster suit.

Lots of stolen cars afterwards.

Screaming teens just ran
down the hill.

# LONG SUBWAY STAIRCASE

Long subway staircase
(without people)
is having such a
luxurious dream.

Awaking to the rush hour,
it suddenly exclaims
"My freedom!"
"My leisure!"

# HYSTERIA OF THE FOREST

Hysteria of the forest awaking
to find itself a prisoner of
the lumber yard, sentenced to
hard labor.

Hypnotized birds cracking whips,
chortling with derision and proud
of their guard uniforms.

# ACCORDIONS

Accordions rudely shoving each other,
trying to get down to the river so
they can be baptized.

The clarinets got there first.

Mistaken by hunters for black moccasins,
they sunk while receiving the last rites.

# A STOIC OWL

A stoic owl is a sombre maestro
conducting a chorale of moonlight.

# IN A DIFFERENT VERSION OF SURPRISE

In a different version of surprise, the
Jack-In-The-Box is savagely beheaded
by disappointed children.

They were expecting something else.

# FORGIVABLE INDIFFERENCE

Forgivable indifference.
Excusable disdain.

The lions nudge one another with
a sarcastic wink.

Watching the tamer stumble as
he drops his whip.

Drunk again.

# THE BUTTERFLY

The butterfly does not remember
being a caterpillar.

It is equally possible that an
arrow regrets hitting the bullseye.

Nature and physics are always
creating mysteries.

# IT'S PISTOLS AT DAWN

It's pistols at dawn for the
pine and oak trees.

A duel to the end (no seconds).

The winner goes straight to the
woodwind maker's shop.

There are many oboes to be made.

# IT'S AS IF THE NIGHT SKY

It's as if the night sky
wears brightness the way
a weary magician puts
on a mask to entertain
a dying child.

Faraway stars looking down at us,
seeing the day's end
as it reveals what we do to
one another.

# PLAGUE OF SORROW

Plague of sorrow
the shadows of
stumbling feet
untied laces trailing the floor
strait jacket buckle dangling
unholy notes of desperate shrieking

until the inevitable
sound
(like an enormous safe falling onto concrete)
of the cell door

clanging shut.

# IN AN IMAGINARY WORLD

In an imaginary world,
the waves unfolding and covering the shore,
commencing the daily shift to high tide and
producing low flat  coverlets that envelope the sand,
become the sheet raised above the head,
after the last breath of the one who
is finally free, like the tiny crab concealed
from the gulls under blankets of foamy sea.

# A JUNKYARD AT MIDNIGHT

A junkyard at midnight frozen with
January snow is the nightmare of
old age.

Loneliness of the staircase finds solace
watching the footsteps of the playing children who
moved away.

# THE INDUSTRY OF A SPIDER

The industry of a spider building its
web is the dream machinery of a child.

Notes of a bassoon are the thickness
of shadows.

Whispering in halls of marble is the
nobility of regret.

# PAPER CROWN FALLING

Paper crown falling off the head of
a child rushing across the room
kicking balloons on his birthday while
a hollow crab shell tumbles across
the sand nudged away by the wind after
ravenous gulls plucked out the flesh.

# HEAVY FURIOUS FLAPPING

Heavy furious flapping of the wings in a
frightened flock abruptly leaving the
ground is the churning wheel noise
puncturing then fading into three a.m.

The smoky locomotive on old tracks.

# THE WAVES

The waves of undulating intonations
during the chorus of voices singing
*Kyrie Eleison*.  The stalks rippling
while hiding creatures listen.  Some
furry darting movements under moonlight.

# ASK FOR THE MAGIC

Ask for magic
and the toy chest scrubs away
shadows from the hallway.  The
child in the last room is what
matters.  A silent puppet smiles
back at you in derision.  Your
shadow gets chased away after
you leave.

# FALLEN ROSE PETALS

Fallen rose petals whisk past the
casket.  Theirs is a momentary
grief.  A nearby fan blows them
towards the chapel door.  Escaping the
sorrow of death.

# A CRUMPLED JESTER COSTUME

A crumpled jester costume with
its colors blocked by shade.

A sombre child reluctantly shaking
off summer's last day.

# NO ONE

No one who contemplates the
mystery of the universe looks
for the secrets in the animating
air that escapes from a collapsing
balloon as it falls to the floor
in a shriveled heap.

# THERE IS AN ELEGANT SILENCE

There is an elegant silence in the
steps of ballet dancers like the
window glass that separates us
from the sparrow's song.

# FROZEN PUDDLES

Frozen puddles in the empty schoolyard
are the sadness of dark asylum corridors.

# THE OLD

The old no longer receive the kind
energy of company,
the same way an unattractive
piece of furniture is kept in a remote
corner of the house.

# EMPTY CONCERT HALL

Empty concert hall dreams of the
music played that night.

# CIRCUS SAWDUST

Circus sawdust, dampened by the saliva
of old tigers, shapes itself into little
pudgy figures.  Later they will dance inside
the exhausted cat's cage.

# WATER AND MIRRORS

Water and mirrors are the language of the soul.
Run your hand through the stream.
Look at the duplicate world of your reflection.
This is how the mysteries are unwrapped.

# WHISPERING CHILDREN

Whispering children in the late afternoon
will forget the lovely matrix of leaf
shadows falling off the ball as they
toss it and catch it and make
secret strategies mouths to ears under
the embracing tree.

# THE STIFLING ENCLOSURE

The stifling enclosure of the confessional
booth produces the quiet stillness and
pathetic helplessness of a beaten dog
too frightened to move or make a sound.

There is a circular wafer of dried blood
near its paw.

# HUMANS WISHING FOR MIRACLES

Humans wishing for miracles.
Big, overwhelming forces of fate
breaking down walls to serve us.

Every night
the excited hungry dog
gazes at his master's hand.
Always the same wonder in his eyes:
watching human fingers
scoop out food from the bag.

# WEALTH OF THE SHADOWS

Wealth of the shadows
spinning and dancing
confusing and misleading
the poverty of our minds.

# TO LOOK THROUGH A WINDOW

To look through a window,
to enter a body of water,
to hear heavy rain and thunder…

Maybe we do not
come out
of our dreams.

Maybe our waking life
rudely pushes
dreams  away.

# PUMPKIN ON A COUNTRY PORCH RAILING

Pumpkin on a country porch,
familiar triangular
cut outs,
the ritual carving to create
grimace
and
fun.

Inside the house
a boy of twelve
is getting into
his devil costume.

Faceless pumpkins still in the patch
give the cold shoulder to these Halloween
preparations.

Jealous over not being picked.

# TINY PUDDLE

Tiny puddle on the side of the road,
almost a pot hole but too
shallow to last much longer,
trying after thunderstorms and wind,
 to survive the
August sun that,
like a scenery change,
suddenly pushes clouds away.

Bathtub faucets turned on full,
even mixture of hot and cold,
din of robust waterfalls
creating waves of cascading bubbles.

By the time she gingerly lowers
her foot to test the heat of
this afternoon bath,
the puddle has evaporated.
It no longer exists.

There is only the little hole and
the crusty dirt dried out by the sun.

# ONE OF THE CEMETERY WORKERS

One of the cemetery workers
turns on a fan in the stuffy
office.  A map showing the
location of her husband's
grave and other funeral papers
fall to the floor as the widow
opens a window to let some
fresh air blow through the
house as she and her
family get ready to be
driven to the burial.

# WE SPEAK OF TIME PASSING

We speak
of time
passing
as if we
own moments.

As if the
moments
were our thoughts.

The way our thoughts belong to us.
The way we own everything that we do.

In reality we own nothing.
We are renters.

Death is the landlord.
Death is the magician
who makes time disappear.

# AN EXCITED GRATEFUL DOG

An excited
grateful
dog
jumps on the lap of the man
in
the wheelchair
joyfully sniffing
the liver from his deceased owner
successfully
transplanted
into
this
stranger.

It is an invisible

joyous
reunion.

# THE IRRATIONAL

The
irrational
yet strangely
disquieting
thought
that we are truly alive
only when
someone
speaks to
us.

# WHAT IS OCTOBER?

for Margaret

What is October?

Smoky air tinged with sweetness of burning leaves.
Scarecrow straw shaking in the sunset wind.
Jittery squirrels' acrobatics across branches.
As if coated with silver make-up the moon has a special glow.

Autumnal colors have evicted the green of summer.
Children sigh over homework books as evening sneaks in.

# SUCH A STRANGE

Such a strange
utterly
gratuitous certainty
in our dreams
that
nothing has been left out.

# HURRYING PAST SPARROW SHADOWS

Hurrying past
sparrow shadows
trembling on the
cold stone wall,
the widow
fumbling and distant
unlocks her door
grateful that she got inside
before the neighbors
had a chance
to ask how
she's been.

# EVERY MOMENT

Every moment that had
content
is now
just
a record of absence.

A few patches
of paw dirt
on the side
of
the pine bookcase.

She jumped up
to get a biscuit
supporting
herself
against the wood.

# SOMEHOW THERE IS HOPEFULNESS

Somehow there is
hopefulness
in silence.

The mind and the body
do not compete
with one another
when all is quiet
and being alive
seems less strange.

# MAYBE THE DISARRANGED
# NEWSPAPER

Maybe the disarranged newspaper
was waiting
for a little boy
to shape
it into a pirate hat.

Perhaps the torn pillowcase
had a secret wish fulfilled
when the little girl
turned it into
her princess cape.

A reprieve of sorts has occurred.

Things touched and used
by adult hands
had been sentenced
to the oblivion
of a garbage can.

Rescued by the inexhaustible
imagination of children,

they are reborn as magical
garments of fantasy.

# WITHOUT TIME PASSING

Without time passing,
there would be no
reason to cherish
a rose.

Scent,
suppleness,
sculptural curves
like the cream
of icing on cakes.

Because time
takes all of this away,
leaving fragile
brittle
red
chips.

Then memory
skips
all of these
dead
barren parts,
restoring to our hearts
all that the rose used to be,
protected by the perfection
of what was.

# ISN'T IT BOTH JOYFUL AND TERRIFYING

Isn't it
both
joyful and terrifying
to return?

Buildings
and
streets that we have not seen
since
childhood.

Especially when
certain things
have not changed.

Crooked streaks of white stippling,
noon light on a wall,
long rows of steep stone steps
in front of a huge public building,
the big trees by the house
where you lived.

Einstein must be right:
past, present, and future
*do* happen at the same time.

The deceptive threads of memory
are the culprits, stitching

an illusory temporal fabric,
making us believe that one
thing happens after another,
disguising the seamless simultaneity
of the world's before and after,
cleverly hiding the past within our perpetual now.

# NOT TO TAKE THE DOG AWAY

Not to take the dog away,
not while she's panting her heavy breaths,
not during her last conscious hours,
not in her final moments of knowing her home.

Someone heard.
Someone granted his wish.
Someone let her die in her house.
Someone lifted her spirit out before her body was taken away.

# IN FRONT OF THE COFFIN

In front of the coffin friends
speak of him.

Remember when…
What about…

In front of the grave workers
bury him.

They don't speak.
The soft earth is silent.

# QUITE A BIT OF THE SUBCONSCIOUS MIND

Quite a bit of the
subconscious mind
must be summoned
in order to evoke
the many nuances
and
the many quirks
of a human face
through the representational
grotesqueries
of
a
mask.

It is so easy to forget
that the purpose of a mask
is not only to conceal.

There must also be some form
of distortion or exaggeration.

Why else would someone wear a mask?

# THERE IS A KIND OF NARCOTIC PU-RITY

There is a kind of
narcotic purity in
the intimacy
and the completeness
of silence.

As if we are enslaved
by a drug, silence does
not serve us.

We serve silence.

After nightfall,
alone in a room,
what a relief
not to hear the
voices and objects
that cluttered our
consciousness throughout the day.
Until we realize we are alone.
Then we feel the numbing
effect of the silence.  It hooks
us with fake peacefulness that
slowly becomes desolation.

# CLOAKS OF SHADOW

Cloaks of
shadow
on
the
cold concrete wall.

Birds' wings
flapping
in
clattering
moonlight of trains.

Winter startled
sparrows
under
El
frightened by noise.


Faintly repeating
iron
wheels
silence
falls under stars.

# IN THE ETERNAL CONFLICT

In the eternal
conflict between
thought and objects,
language is a reluctant referee.

# WHY DOES IT SEEM

Why
does it seem as though
the windowsill
has suddenly earned
greater admiration
from the sun
after a new plant
is brought over
to be nurtured in
the glow and the heat?

# THE STRANGE UNEXPECTED COMFORT

The strange
unexpected
comfort from dreams quickly
draining out of our morning
wakefulness,
allowing the "real" world
to successfully pretend
it is there
and
we are
in it.

# FLICKER OF MIND

Flicker of mind
in the temptation of now.

Shadows,
shapes,
patterns planning
visits of later.

Children's dreams
in rooms of play,

cluttered by
the things of today.

Dreamscapes
with clear horizons
catching the clarity
of delightful fun.


The genius for abandon gradually
leaves its first and only home:
nestled behind a sleeping child's eyes.

Never looking back as it crosses
strict adult skies remembering when it was
nestled behind a sleeping child's eyes.

# JUST LIKE A LOVING PARENT

Just like a loving parent
who places a colorful, tinkling
mobile above an infant's crib,

suppose the creator of our
universe has done the same
thing with time and space?

Pointing with wonder,
reaching with curiosity,
the infant is amazed at
this apparent world, floating
so magically above his head.

Endless planets and stars,
such a magnificent gift
from the one who creates.


Our amazement?
At an apparent world?

Floating so magically
above our heads.

# OF THE LITTLE THAT CAN BE SAID

Of the little
that
can
be
said,

there should be
more.
At
least

something about the
look
of
courageous

acceptance and
dignified
resignation
to
his fate.  Sitting
proudly,
having
his

picture taken before
being
destroyed
with

hundreds of other
discarded
dogs,
this

large statuesque hound
sits
perfectly
still,

calmly staring into
the
photographer's
camera.

Somehow there is
a
terrible
feeling

that he knows
what
is
about

to happen.  Somehow
he
calmly
accepts

his fate with
the
grace

of
a martyr.  Somehow
the human world
is diminished by his death.

# OUR PAST

Our past
and all of the memories
in it
do not truly belong
to our review
or recollection.

They belong to the
solemn
silent
world of the indexical,
the living before
of what we are and
what we did.

Decades of lives
and innumerable steps
walking up and down
a stone staircase
more than a century old.

Like a scooped out slice
of spinning wet clay,
there is the smoothened
slope of the stone step,
worn down during the
years, after the climbing
and descending of so
many who are gone.

# THE IDEA OF NOTHING

The idea of nothing
becomes a search
for content.

Emptied rooms of
houses without
inhabitants.

Embers mild glow
surrounded by suffocating
ash.

Hands no longer waving
at a vanished ship
absorbed by the horizon.


Sounds of children's shouts
tumbling and toys fade into the
numb memories of gray haired parents.

The face of nothing smirks at the mirror.
The mirror grows dim and hinders our search.

# THE MYSTERY OF KNOWING

The mystery of knowing
future things is perhaps
hinted at by thinking
of an infinite number of
film projectors lined up in
a row.

All of the people, events,
objects, and places of
our lives are shown.

Each projector shows the
same film.  Each film
shows the same things.

Yet every film has a
different ending.  Every
ending is equally real.
All the reality of the
last moments of our
lives is equally present.

Every ending that is possible
is happening at the same time.

The only certainty is that
such simultaneity is unknowable
and that the future is always
being born without being conceived.

# AN AFTERIMAGE

An afterimage is
the most sincere
charlatan.

The recording
equipment of our senses,
unfailingly, exquisitely
tricked, as we involuntarily recreate
something
from the world.

Closing our eyes does
not
erase
the candle on the table,
the shell on the shore,
the child in the meadow.

Our brain is haunted,
if only for several seconds,
by the superb forgery
of a flawless imposter.

Like a listless jester,
the reality of what we see loses its charm,
as though it has died and is forever gone,
resurrected for a moment on the magic screen of the mind,
freed from life and its prison of time.

# THE IMAGINATION

The imagination is an
unnatural phenomenon
in the world of
things and thought.

Things demand to be
accepted for what
they are.

Thought believes
it has the privilege
to make changes.

The irrational bridge
between things and thought
is provided by the imagination.

How else could we say
that tiny shadows
of a sparrow, rubbing
its breast with its beak,
have the same jittery motion
as the nervous fingers of a husband,
petting his dead wife's hair
with disbelief and grief?

# THE FIXED EMPTY STARE

The fixed empty stare
of the
eyes of the dead
does not mock the living.

There is no emotion there,
like a wrinkled rubber
mask held
up by the fingers, dangling
with black soul less sockets.

Just as the mask has lost
its human occupant, the one
who looked with life through
these frozen
orbs of pupil and iris
is now ethereal mist.


Yet we cannot resist
the need to see the dead as they were.
A lifeless costume
falls to the floor in a
disarranged crumpled heap.

An eyeless mask conveys
neither praise nor condemnation.

And the open eyes of the dead make
us think of a cinematic freeze frame.

They were in the middle of doing something,
we say to ourselves, and the film
suddenly stopped.

# IT MAY BE

It may be that
objects are always
hiding
from scrutiny.

Shadows may be weary
of the dread we
ascribe to them in
our notions and narratives.

Reflections may resent the
inflections we impose upon
their meaning in our moments.

Roses may be understandably
indifferent to the imprint
of love and devotion
we ceaselessly borrow from
their flawless form.

Stars may learn to
neglect the night,
to remove themselves
from our wistful gaze,
to extinguish our reverie
and delight.

Coffins remain oblivious to our thoughts and our deeds.
They collect the final debt regardless of our needs.

# FEAR OF THE MOMENT

Fear of the moment
that will be our last.
We reach for reassurance
and try to resurrect the past.
Limping thoughts need prosthetics,
our minds are blank movie screens.
All of life seems an obscure text
refusing to explain what it means.
We think we have gleefully kidnapped love
but the exquisite ransom is never paid.
Our dreams become circus stilts letting
us pretend we walk through life unafraid.
There is little to possess and
far less to treasure.
We are like blind conductors
without podium, baton or measure.

We weep because our living flesh
is all that we truly believe.
We sleep so that our carefree souls
can prepare for the day they must leave.

# THERE IS A SENSE OF PALPABLE REMORSE

There is a sense
of palpable remorse
and solitude in the
faraway call of a fog horn.

As though a forlorn bassoon,
separated from the orchestra,
was helplessly trying
to identify its unmapped location.

Sea mist weaves opaque curtains
of silence, surrounding the

salty blackness of
dense, still water.

Thick digits of gray air resist and resent
the sonorous intrusion of this
invisible interloper.
The destiny of ships is
in their hands.
Their filmy fingers will
shape the night's fate.

# ALOOFNESS MAY BE UNINTENTIONAL

Aloofness may be
unintentional, but
like a stuffy diplomat
or the unapproachable aspect
of a royal personage,
the owl has earned a chilly
reputation for being
inaccessible, remote, indifferent.

Of course, we like to think
these are the esoteric
ingredients of wisdom.
Surely, in order to be wise,
the owl must detach itself from
folly, amusement, giddiness.

What if his talent for
seeing in the night
allowed him to enter our dreams?
He could fly through
our fanciful slumber, visiting the
fantastic landscapes we create.

But seriousness and an unshakable
commitment to duty keep the stoical owl on his
solitary perch, scanning the field for
mice, meditating in soft moonlight,
sedate, satisfied, serene.

# CHILDREN ARE NOT AFRAID

Children are not afraid
to answer the wind
with their shouts and
grunts as they run
towards the ball
nudging one another
as they play and
fall out of breath
in the grass.

Laughing young voices
breathless in the sweeping
fall air that wraps itself
around their heads
asking if they are happy.

Adults hurry past the playground
hats in place coats buttoned
scarves wrapped around throats.

They have not spoken to the wind in years.
They have nothing to say.

# IT IS AS THOUGH

It is as though
there are moments
when objects reluctantly
reveal their secrets.

The motionless rubber ball,
lying on the floor in
late afternoon sun,
casting a spherical shadow
next to the stained dog's bed.

Incontinence preceded death.
Death was followed by the
removal of objects.
Objects such as the ball and
the bed.

Like a flimsy toupee for a
featureless mannequin,
there is a little tuft of
hair and dust clinging to
the ball, stuck in place
from dried urine and saliva.

It rolled against the inside of
the metal ash can after it
was thrown away.

# THE GRAND IMMOBILITY OF THE SPHINX

The grand immobility
of the Sphinx,
staring in unchanging stone.

Like the inaccessibility
of an indifferent heart,
or the venomous entanglement
of wrestling scorpions.

Love unrequited, like the
monolithic monument, is
best symbolized by stasis,
that which cannot move or
evolve beyond a given point.

Just as the Sphinx, without
volition or compassion, watches
the scorpions die,
the numb recipient of unwanted
love reveals nothing, keeping
secrets in solemn silence.

# WOUNDS THAT PUNCTURE

Wounds that puncture
or cut flesh, from
pistol or blade, can
be restored by
surgeon's skill.

Words left unspoken through the
drudgery of time
and the inconvenience
of life become insidious infections.

The wild gangrenous torment
of endless sorrow and regret.

Death has forever removed the moment
when heartfelt things could have been said.

The first shovelful of loose earth
slides across the polished casket.

# JUST AS MEMORY FLEETINGLY RECREATES

Just as memory
fleetingly recreates
the past, flying
little kites of
what was across
our muddled minds,
music invisibly delivers
the same kind of
emotional gifts.

Belonging to the air,
without body or hands,
music reaches for us,
the mystical offspring
of composers' paper
and musicians' mastery.

It is as if there is
no home or mode
of being for the
sounds we cherish
except as ambassadors
from a magical dimension,
fully and beautifully alive
within us, no longer burdened
by the heaviness of form
or the tyranny of time.

# SLICK WITH FRESH SLIPPERY BLOOD

Slick with fresh slippery blood,
the long metal cutting table
glistens in the dawn sun as
the bustling fish market opens.

Flailing thick salmon tail furiously
smacks the aluminum.  Streaks
of red stain the worker's white apron.

What was a superbly designed
combination of rudder and engine,
moving and guiding the fish,
now beats the air like an aimless sleepwalker.

Death throes continue after decapitation.
Scattered iridescent scales.  Myriad blood bubbles.

Blank staring eyes.

# THERE IS A PLACE IN THE MIND

There is a place
in the mind
where touch
mixed with thought
turns the delightful smoothness
of marble into
a womblike reassurance
that despair is not inevitable.

# WHAT A MAGNIFICENT, SURREAL IDEA!

What a magnificent, surreal idea!

It is as though we are
living recording devices,
the most sophisticated movie camera,
walking, breathing, sitting, hearing,
filming every second of our conscious
physical lives.

Our dreams are woven out
of what's left on the
cutting room floor.

# THERE IS A KIND OF HOSTILITY

There is a kind of hostility
in grating, loud noise.
Almost as though the objects
responsible for the sudden clatter
are in cahoots with the imagination.
The grinding motor of the
lawnmower across the street
can mean only one thing:
the man mowing his lawn has
murdered his wife in a ghastly,
grisly way.

His calmness shields him from scrutiny.
The neighbors don't suspect a thing.

# CHILDHOOD IS AN EXCLUSIVE CLUB

Childhood is an exclusive club.
Maturity permanently ends
membership, cancelling all rights
and privileges.  To join, one must
slay dragons, marry the prince, and
above all, be blissfully unburdened
by tomorrow.  Eventually, every
member mournfully hands in their star
dust and magic carpets in exchange
for alarm clocks, offices,
and memories.

# A SUMMER NIGHT

A summer night is a long
forgotten lover, the enchantment
of starlight, all of the delights
purchased by the senses,
licked curves of a child's ice cream cone,
an enticing hint of the texture
of paradise, ocean music in every key,
all the delivered promises buried by
winter's deceit, all the glistening fur
of rhythmically dancing wheat, all the
anointed aspirations of all the souls who meet.

# THE MIRRORS OF MOMENTS

The mirrors of moments
turned into a private gallery,
photographs in rows,
thick album heavy,
pages turned slowly,
images frozen,
inhabiting the past,
we used to belong there,
but that was a dream
unwittingly recorded
by a dispassionate camera
capturing objects and humans
with precision and indifference.

# WHAT IF...

What if the endless,
untiring waves of the ocean,
constantly unfolding,
always reaching with innocent energy,
were made to remind
us of children rushing through rooms,
arms outstretched
in the sparkling anticipation of
hugs generously given and happily received?

# BLACK COSSACK SKIRT

Black cossack skirt
brusquely slapping
stone in cemetery
wild wind.

Biretta twirls across
fresh grave, suddenly
knocked to the ground
by rude gusts of air.

Child's casket and the
hope to have
mortal mysteries unwrapped,
left behind, as
parents leave, accompanied
by perfunctory blessings
from the priest who retrieved his hat.

# **TUMULTS**

Tumults
of rapid pelting rain
are like thousands of
shouting hypnotists
making us think
only of what is inside
dry
and warm.

# STILLNESS OF A LIZARD

Stillness of a lizard
as if it is stone
as if it is a photograph
that it will no longer move
that it is an imitation of itself
the motionlessness of death
the immobility of death
a feeling that nothing can change
a feeling that finality is eternal
that is the feeling
leaving the chapel
walking away from the casket
walking away from the body
that has the
stillness of a lizard.

# THOUGHTS OF WHITE AND BLUE

Thoughts of white
and blue, a piece
of wood and a canvas patch,
as the man in an old
sailor cap hurries across
the street.

Looking over
his shoulder at this
nautical fellow,
thinking thoughts of sea and surf,
the little boy decides
that there must be a
lighthouse waiting for
this man who is walking so
briskly and has already
disappeared into the chaos
of rushing pedestrians
across the street.
People should stop and politely
*greet him!* the child thinks
to himself. *Someone in their*
family could be on one of the
*ships he guides.*

He tugs his mother's hand to share this
revelation but she has to finish her
shopping and hurries towards
the supermarket with her son in tow.

# MYSTERY AND CERTAINTY

Mystery
and
certainty,
like schizophrenic
Siamese
twins,
foster one another
even
as they fester,
forever competing,
never meeting
or truly seeing
things
eye
to
eye.

Mystery always leaves early,
taking all of the answers away
but giving humanity the endless
thrill of wonder and awe.

Certainty uses its steel strong
jaws to grind away speculation's
fanciful fruits, while calming
irrational fears with sobering truths.

Late at night, as the bar is about to close,
Mystery and Certainty make a toast
to mankind: *Let imagination always seek,*
*even if it does not always find.*